TEA

HOW TO RESPECT
PERSONAL SPACE

The Physical and Psychological
Body Boundaries on
Consent, Respect, Feelings, Choices
And Relationship With Others

COPYRIGHT

author, addressed "Attention: Permissions to copy," at the address below.

EMAIL:

BELLASTARDOM101@GMAIL.COM

DEDICATION

I specially dedicate this book to all children worldwide including my dearest daughter, Bella (Jnr).

TABLE OF CONTENTS

CHAPTER ONE

INTRODUCTION

What is Personal Space?

Personal space refers to the physical or psychological distance between two or more people in a social, family, work environment, or society in general. Personal space can be compared to the air between your body and an invisible shield, or bubble; you have created around yourself for any relationship.

The distance between you and your bubble can vary from one person to another, depending on various factors, like how well you know the person, your closeness to that person, how much you trust him or her, and your culture.

Personal Space in Children

Therefore, personal space is a social skill that every parent or guardian needs to imbibe in their children right from the elementary level. Children need to learn, practice, and grow along with the skills.

This is paramount, as it will help children in their social interactions and engagements with people. More importantly, it will help them in forming a good relationship with people of their peer-level, and adults who are older than they are. It will also be of advantage to them in avoiding unnecessary embarrassments in the society, which might take a toll on their parent's parenting skills. An uncultured child will definitely bring shame and reproach to the parents.

According to Neetu from St. Xavier's High School, she believes that: **"Children are into the habit of hugging, kissing, touching, and incessant movement as they speak,"**

Even though we find these habits sweet and encourages physical touch at home in showing love, kids need to be taught about no-touch-no-intrusion practices outside.

Imagine a boy of 5 touching women he sees outside in a sexually pervasive manner (except for children who have Attention Deficit Hyperactivity Disorder (ADHD)); people around will definitely blame the parents for not teaching the boy some proper etiquettes and personal space. Good personal space in children also helps them to stay safe anywhere they are, thereby making them avoid closeness to harmful people.

It's a natural feeling to be comfortable when people give us personal space; we tend to respect the person more as against those who intrude into your privacy anyhow.

There are some popular beliefs on how much space is appropriate in a particular situation. Therefore, the amount of personal space we want as an individual varies according to the circumstances or situation on the ground.

So, personal space changes according to these three factors, which are:

- **Who you are with**
- **What you are doing**
- **Where you are**

For kids, personal space can be the same size for everybody. And they seem to think that everybody has the same space bubble as they have. This is most common in children who have Attention Deficit Hyperactivity Disorder (ADHD). These type of children may approach you and sit on your laps, play with your hair, hug you unnecessarily, tap you indiscriminately, touch your body in inappropriate places.

As we all know that this is inappropriate and uncultured behavior for many people. So, when kids do these things to teachers or adults, we generally know how to handle the situation and correct the child's behaviors. But if this happens between two kids, when a child intrudes into the other child's personal space, it results in to fight.

Children get uncomfortable, angry, and annoyed when other children get into their personal space. So, this is why it is necessary to teach children what good personal space is. And how to tell if they are already invading into other person's personal space, also if they are, the solutions to correct it.

HOW TO CREATE PERSONAL SPACE (ACTIVITIES AND RESULTS)

Firstly, there are two types of personal space. Tangible space, which is the physical space around us that we can see with our eyes. While the other one, which is intangible space, is psychological or emotional space.

It is so easy to teach on maintaining distance as you approach, communicate, and interact with others. This is tangible or physical personal space.

But the problem seems to arise whenever we want to teach about intangible personal space such as; respecting other's decisions to be alone, understanding body language, asking personal questions, etc.

These problems lead to the invention of these activities to

teach children about personal space in a stylish way to add fun to learning. It's cool; you can try them out with your kids.

CHAPTER TWO

KNOW YOUR BODY

This activity is to help the parents or guardians of toddlers, especially.

You should start by introducing your children to their various body parts and the use of those body parts during conversations. Therefore, they will understand more about the term "Personal Space" through this.

WHAT YOU NEED

- A large piece of chart
- A marker or felt a pen
- Your child/children

ACTIVITIES (USING CHART FOR BODY IDENTIFICATION)

- Lay the chart on the floor like a rug.

- Ask your child/children to lie down on the chart and trace his/her/their body outline.
- Hang the outline on the wall
- Point to the parts of the body and explain the use of hands, face, and feet.
- Explain and analyze that the idea behind body language comes from using the body during communication.

RESULTS

- It's exciting for a child/children to see his/her/their body outlined.

- It's learning by a fun way of introducing the various parts of the body and getting the child/children to listen.

- It helps parents in introducing the concept of body language to their child/children at a young age.

CHAPTER THREE

THE HULA LOOP TEST

It is good to visualize the concept of personal space for children. Since children can maintain a relationship with other people according to their parents' instructions. So it is necessary to tell them how to maintain their space in the midst of people, as well as when they are alone.

WHAT YOU NEED

- A hula hoop or a meter-long rope
- A piece of chalk

ACTIVITIES (USING HULA HOOP ILLUSTRATION)

- Let your child/children wear the hula hoop around his/her/their waist. If you are using rope, tie the ends of the rope together so that the child/children can hold it as a belt near his/her/their waist.

- Stand close to him/her/them so that your body touches the hula hoop. Using the chalk, mark your position on the floor. For the rope, the position is as far as the diameter of the rope.

- Ask your child/children if he/she/they feel(s) comfortable depending on the understanding of the words.

- Then, enter the hula hoop/rope belt so that the two of you are inside the hoop together individually.
- Mark your position.
- Now ask again if he/she/they feel(s) comfortable. Since you are the parent, your child/children will be comfortable with the closeness.
- Explain how this comfort means comfortable personal space.

RESULTS

- You can initiate discussions about personal space in regards to safety when you show your child/children the positions of the mark that you have made on the floor.

- As said earlier, when parents are closer to their children, they feel safe, but when strangers are near, they feel otherwise. This is why nobody should be allowed inside the space of the hula hoop/rope circle except the parents.

- Now you can ask your child to imagine being inside the hoops every time, this definitely works in visualizing and teaching personal space to children.

CHAPTER FOUR

USE OF EMOJIS

- It seems the eyes and distance says a lot about comfort.

- Children can be taught to understand emotions and

comfort just by looking at other people's eyes. They should figure out other people's comfort rather than sensing it.

Below is an activity that illustrates this better.

WHAT YOU NEED

- A printed paper having different emojis on it. (these are the icons commonly used in chatting on social media like Whatsapp, Facebook, Instagram, etc. to convey different moods or feelings)

ACTIVITIES (IDENTIFICATION OF EMOJIS)

- Show the paper full of emojis (short for icons that show

moods or feelings) and ask your child/children which one shows anger.

- He/she/they will definitely know and point to the angry icon.
- Ask your child/children how he/she/they know(s) for sure. Is it the eyes?
- Also, ask him/her/them to identify emojis for excitement, sad, cry, happy, etc.

RESULTS

- The eyes and hands are the most significant features that display emotion, and understanding this emotion lays the foundation for understanding personal space.

- You can also tell your child/children that keeping a distance during conversations and knocking before entering are forms of the same concept of personal space,"

Try it; it works.

CHAPTER FIVE

EAVESDROPPER

- Listening to other people's conversations or discussions is also a means of invading personal space. This is why we need to teach children about respecting personal space in the sense of minding one's business.

- It is common to let our children hear our conversations with people on the phone, which they believe it's a good thing to listen to. But we need to teach them not to eavesdrop on people's conversations outside, and this is part of respecting personal space.

WHAT YOU NEED

- A toy phone

ACTIVITIES (FAKE PHONE CALLING)

- Tell your child/children to make a faux phone call using a toy phone to call Mum/Dad or anyone else he/she/they wish to talk to.

- When he/she/they speak(s), try and get very close and listen to the conversation. Making sure your behavior disrupts the child/children and interrupts the conversation.

•

- When the child/children get(s) irritated or throw a tantrum, tell him/her/them that listening to other people's conversation is an intrusion of personal space and leads to irritation.

RESULTS

- This will make your child/children know(s) the idea behind not listening in on other people's conversations or at least not being too close while a conversation is ongoing.

- Whether he/she/they follow the rules when you are on the phone is not guaranteed.

But try this, it works.

CHAPTER SIX

LETTERS READING

- Children are often fond of reading letters, notes, or personal journals you made on the family computer. This constitutes an invasion of personal space too.

WHAT YOU NEED

- A pen
- A sheet of paper

ACTIVITIES (WRITING A FAUX LETTER)

- This one needs mum and dad to be together.

- Sit down with your child/children and announce

that one of you is writing a letter to him/her/them.

- Do as if you are writing a letter to your child/children as he/she/they look at you.

- Once you finished writing the letter, fold it, and place it in front of your child/children.

- Before your child/children pick(s) up the letter, the other parent (one who did not write the letter) should take the letter and pretend to be reading it.

- Definitely, your child/children might throw tantrums or become uncomfortable with this.

RESULTS

- As you give the letter back to your child/children, explain the discomfort that he/she/they felt when the letter was read by the parent first.
- Then explain to him/her/them that the discomfort is due to

invasion of privacy, which is the reason why reading someone's letter/journal/personal note is not a good thing to do.

CHAPTER SEVEN

BASIC RULES OF PERSONAL SPACE YOUR CHILDREN NEEDS TO KNOW

1. Don't touch anyone you don't know.

2. Don't cut in front of people in line.

3. Don't lean over someone's shoulder to read something unless invited.

4. Stand at least 4 feet away from a person unless you know him or her well.

5. Take a step back when someone leans away from you, there are chances you are in the person's space which makes him or her uncomfortable.

6. Don't fling your arm around someone's shoulder unless you know the person very well.

7. Never go through other people's personal belongings.

8. Never smack anyone on the back unless you know the person very well.

9. Don't allow your dog to go to the bathroom of other people's property.

10. Never enter a room or office without knocking first.

There are some specific skills that need to be applied when teaching children new social skills; this is necessary to make it enforceable.

These skills are:

- **PATIENCE**
- **CONSISTENCY**

- **COMMENDATION**

-

PATIENCE: This is a must-have skill when dealing with children, as it is known that preschool children have a short attention span and may need to be reminded many times of the same thing.

CONSISTENCY: If it is not okay to barge in the restroom without knocking, the rule should be applicable to everyone in the family. And if there is any change in the rules, let the child/children know.

Family rules can be somehow flexible to allow room for normal development, so when there is inconsistency in the rules, the child/children get(s) confused.

COMMENDATION: You need to be positive and give compliments when you see your child/children learning fast and applying the rules of personal space. For instance, when he/she/they asked for permission before entering the restroom, commend him/her/them. It helps in maintaining the rules of personal space.

CONCLUSION

Personal space is all about how close you can come to people in different situations without letting them feel uncomfortable. Some children learn about personal space without being taught, while in some children, it is unclear to them about personal space. Alternatively, some children might need more personal space than we expect, and they sometimes feel upset when others invade their space.

So, as a parent, guardian, teacher, you can help your child/children to learn, practice, and grow along with by following all the ideas and practical examples contained in this book. I wish you and your child/children a lovely and healthy relationship.

OTHER BOOKS BY THE AUTHOR

You can also get these books written by me (Bella Stardom) which are:

TEACHING CHILDREN HOW TO RESPECT PERSONAL SPACE.

It is available in both Kindle and Paperback, kindly click on the image or the links below to grab a copy.

Kindle:

https://www.amazon.com/dp/B08
3K56D4R

Paperback: **Also Available**

ANGER MANAGEMENT FOR KIDS

WITH ANGER ISSUES

Kindle:

https://www.amazon.com/dp/B08
28HF81N

Paperback:

https://www.amazon.com/dp/1670
899292

CONTACT THE AUTHOR

For any enquiries, suggestions, feedbacks and any other information; you can contact the author by email at:

BELLASTARDOM101@GMAIL.COM

NOTES

Made in the USA
Middletown, DE
01 November 2023